Davanzo inc.

- BASED ON A TRUE STORY -

and actual events.

Jerome Davanzo

561-951-1117

Davanzo inc.

Jerome Davanzo
Davanzo inc.

Published by Spines

ISBN: 979-8-89691-389-4

Hi, my name is Jerome Davanzo. I was born in Youngstown, Ohio, in 1966 to parents Carmine,2 times Golden Glove Champion and Loretta Rabosky. Carmine, my father, was born to parents Frank Davanzo and Marry Mancinni, who are sisters to the son of the original Lenny Boom Boom Mancinni. Whose son Raymond Boom

Boom Mancini, who killed the Korean boxer Duk Koo Kim in the World Championship Boxing Bout in Las Vegas in 1982.

one

SPORTS ANNOUNCER

"And here is the 23-year-old challenger, and there is the 21-year-old Raymond Boom Boom Mancinni, and he scored Mancinni landed a combination sending Kim to the canvas, and it's all over Raymond Boom Boom Mancinni with a 14th round knock out of the challenger Duk Koo Kim what a fight what a finish in Las Vegas Nevada and the handlers of Boom Boom Mancinni into the ring congratulating their champion his certain success of the WBA crown. Well, I don't know for certain what he expected today. We'll find out when we talk to him. I gotta believe he was surprised by the ability and stamina of Duk KOO Kim, but he showed again he is a worthy champion, and his happy father, Lenny, saw his son score the late knockout of Duk Koo Kim from South Korea. It came at 19 seconds of the 14th round, a tough combination that set up a right hand that sent him flying; there is the champion Raymond Boom Boom Mancinni. I have to believe he's glad this fight is over right now. He had his hands full today. We're going to go back to that 14th round: a right and a left just missed him, and a big right hand from Boom Boom and Kim was finished; at that point, he tried to get up, but he had nothing left a big right hand. And there is the champion Ray Boom Boom Mancinni, and so he has retained his WBA championship. And we'll be back to talk to the champion Ray Boom Boom Mancinni. Let's go to New York and talk to Bret Musberger when CBS Sports continues. We are back in Las Vegas with the champion Ray Boom Boom Mancinni. And they have taken the challenger, a very game Duk Koo Kim, out of the ring on a stretcher and apparently taking him to the nearby hospital where he will be checked out (3 days later, he dies from the injuries he sustained from the fight after that the WBA changed the rules forever from 14 round fights to 12 round fights) also three brothers Carmine, Rocco and Anthony incidentally Rocco was named after Rocky Marciano."

I was raised in a primarily boxing family and a Mafia family; of course, the two coincided in those times.1968 moved to Boca Raton, FL, where I attended St. Joan of Arc Catholic School.

(Show here in kindergarten with a teacher on a chalkboard)

TEACHER

"a b c d e f g h, etc. Tell me what you think of me."

two

1972 moved to Rochester, Mn.

TOWN OF MAYO CLINIC, while in Rochester, Mn.

(Insert Film of me growing up)

I attended the 1st through 12th grade. During my time there, the Mayo Clinic was the place where all the astronauts came to train.

(Show g-force machine)

The movie stars, even the Shaw of Iran who had given me this gold medallion when I was 14 and I wore it around my neck with a shoestring and of course every Mafia boss on the planet, as the Mayo Clinic was the most advanced clinic/hospital in the world. Needless to say, as I grew up, my mom used to say.

MOM

"Boys, your father's friends are coming for dinner."

She had no idea they were all the Mafia bosses from all over the country, from NY to Las Vegas, Chicago, Miami, etc. So, in turn, it made my brothers and I the most connected people on the planet. We were the Davanzo boys, sons of Carmine Davanzo and his Brother, my uncle Mike Davanzo, from Youngstown, Ohio (crime town USA), where my family owned a junkyard to crush bodies.

(Show junkyard crushing car)

Funeral home to incinerate bodies.

[Show funeral home]

The liquor store next to our restaurant, where the slot machines, roulette tables, and poker tables were played, and of course, where the family meetings took place, even had Congressman Jim Traficant, who at that time was the sheriff of Mahoning County as well as the chief of police of Youngstown, and who was a partner in the restaurant we owned; nothing happened in that town we didn't know about. We were "Murder Inc." No hit on any member of the Italian Mafia was carried out unless contracted by my family.

three

1982, Rochester, MN.

SO I'M 16 years old, and my boys and I get busted smoking weed by the police. I was a minor, and it was my first offense, so the judge sentenced me to two months of community service. I chose to work off at the local recreation center, which had an indoor Olympic-sized swimming pool, a hockey arena and several other amenities. I got assigned to work with the gentleman who ran the Zamboni. He would scrape the ice rink, and I would hose down the ice with hot water and wash it down the drain. We became friends and kept in contact.

So now I'm 17, and my father and I are traveling back and forth between Ohio and Florida, running the businesses. By the way, I did finish high school at the same time. I had rented a 70-acre farm with a three-bedroom house and two barns on the property. My brother Carmine had a band with his buddies, so I would hire them to play shows out at the farm. This was my first business. I would shoot a 400lb pig, butcher him and cook it for 2 days on my homemade BBQ grill, then purchase 10-15 kegs of beer and throw a party every other weekend. I would get the ice for kegs at the recreation center from my buddy who drove the Zamboni. Wow, 2000 plus guests every other weekend at $5 per guest was $20,000.00 a month in my pocket minus expenses at $4000 per month, Not bad for a 17-year-old, plus I had all the hot chicks from 3 high schools in town and all the high schools in the small rural towns in the area. I loved the girls from Lourdes High, the Catholic High School in town. The good old days when it was Ricky, Craig, Jonny and I. What a time to grow up, the 80s. Shit now that I think about it, I was banging the college girls from town as well.

Jerome

> "Oh no, you girls are free. You're all beautiful. Save your money for your wedding dresses" "Pacasos."

And there she was, Lisa Crowson, my first love in the 6th grade. I was 11 years old; we used to play "spin the bottle together, my first kiss. After the 6th grade, she moved with her family to New York City to become a child model, and I hadn't seen her since. She looked at me, and I stared back at her. She ran to me and jumped up and wrapped her arms around my neck and her legs around my waist, and we held each other for what seemed like an eternity, and we both wept with joy; we fell to the ground and rolled around laughing, and she said.

Lisa C

> "You"

Jerome

> "My Love"

You couldn't separate us with a stick for the rest of the night.

Rick Funk

"Look at Romey. I've never seen him like that."

Johny Day

"Oh my God."

Craig Flick

"Is he crying? Who is that girl?"

Rick

"That's Lisa Crowsen. Romey loves her. They were kids together. Let them go. Anyone who even looks at her funny, Romy will kill them."

Craig

"Are they holding hands?"

Ricky

"I'm telling you, bro, back off this one."

I never saw or heard from her again, but it was the best night of my life. When she had to leave to go home at 7:00 a.m., we both cried again and held each other's hands for over an hour as we watched the sunrise. This time, we got to say goodbye.

Craig and I also grew weed on the farm and sold joints at $3 each. We would sell a minimum of 1,500 joints per party, adding another $9,000.00 per month to our income. We had the weed for sale at all times; we supplied several distributors in town, which knocked our income out of the park. We even sold it to one of our teachers at our high school. We were spoiled rich kids who didn't have to use our parents' money. Yeah, we were Boy Scouts. How do you think we got started in organized crime? I was a master grower before I got into the family business of importing flowers, and Ricky, Craig and Jonny were in charge when I was out of town on business with my father. After all, the family business was my future.

four

1984, Youngstown, Ohio, at a family restaurant.

Uncle Mike

"Here are your orders, son. Just do it like we taught you."

He handed me two folders with plane tickets and instructions, which I burned later.

Jerome

"Yes, sir."

Now I'm at the airport, landing in Chicago. It's my first hit, and I'm really nervous; I rent a car and proceed to the address in my folder. I'm sitting in the car, looking at the picture outside. The target is a rat. His turning states evidence on Chicago boss Joseph Ferriola, who is on the witness protection program. There are two FBI agents outside sitting in their car. I am dressed in all black and pull my face mask down. I'm also wearing my bullet-proof vest. I approach the home with extreme caution; I slip past the two agents and enter the house. I pull out my 38 semi-auto in one hand and two sticks of dynamite in the other. I proceed up the stairs to the second floor and enter the bedroom where the target is sleeping. I hold the sticks of dynamite to the barrel of my gun and pull the trigger, hitting my target in the forehead at the same time, igniting the dynamite from the flash. Now, the agents heard my shot and are now running toward the front door. KABOOM, the explosion goes off and blasts the two agents back 20 feet; by the time they came through, I was long gone.

(Plane landing in Las Vegas. I'm exiting the plane.)

STUARDEST

“Welcome to Las Vegas.”

I nod my head and smile.

Jerome

"Thank you"

I proceed to the locker, take out the key, open the locker, retrieve a 45mm handgun and place it in my possession. I proceed to the business of the next target; the target is sitting at the bar talking to the man next to him. It’s 10:00 am, and no customers are at the establishment at this time. I walk in, put the gun up to the target’s head, pull the trigger, the gun goes off, and the bullet goes through the target’s head, splattering brains on the second man as he turns his head, the bullet pierces the second man in his eyeball, and both men drop dead.

Youngstown, Ohio, at a restaurant.

Dad

"Jerome, what the fuck happened in Vegas? You killed a made man. Do you know what that means? They're going to kill you now. You've got us in a real predicament here, son."

Jerome

"Pops, it was an accident. The bullet went through the target's head and into the eyeball of the other guy. Shit, shit, shit, I knew this was a dangerous job."

Uncle Mike enters the room.

Uncle Mike

"Oh look, who's back? Well, you're a man now; we're going to have to make you a made man now, especially with your fuck up. I got a lot of fast talking to do to get you out of this, but this is what we have to do to get your protection; right now, your father and I are the only ones who know you pulled the trigger in Las Vegas."

Jerome

"Yeah, I got the job done."

Dad

> "Yeah, I should smack you so fucking hard; the police picked you up for speeding in Miami."

Later the same night, driving down a road in Lowville, an outskirt of Youngstown, my dad, Uncle Mike and I.

Jerome

> "Pops, stop at the liquor store. I need to get a bottle of Jack."

Dad

> "Ok son"

We proceeded through the liquor store; there was a bum outside the liquor store.

Bum

> "Can you spare some change?

Jerome

> "Yeah, here's $500. Get yourself cleaned up and get a job."

Bum

> "Thank you. Thank you. God bless, thank you."

Jerome

"One more stop, Pa, my girl's house."

We drive to my girl's home. I get out of the car and run upstairs.

Girl Friend

"Jerome, I'm pregnant, and it's yours."

I reach into my pocket and pull out a wad of cash, setting the bottle on the counter.

Jerome

"I'll be back, and here, get rid of it."

Throwing a bunch of cash at her, I proceed back down the stairs.

I was walking toward the Cadillac with my father and Uncle in it when, all of a sudden, an SUV pulled up and started unloading an AK-47 into the car. I pull out my handgun and start unloading it into the SUV as it screams away. I approach the Cadillac and grab my father in my arms as he passes. I look up and shout.

Jerome

"Noooooooo"

Go to the funeral of Father and Uncle Mike; it's a big Mafia funeral. All the bosses are there from all over the country: Genovese, Castellanos, Joey Naples, John Gotti, etc. Anthony, my brother, is the priest who is doing the service.

Outside, church bells are chiming, and you can hear the light sound of the organ playing inside. There is a slow flow of people entering the church.

(Priest reciting the Lord's Prayer.)

Anthony

"Our Father, who art in heaven, hallowed be thy name; thy kingdom come, thy will be done, etc."

Joey Napels

"Sorry for your loss, Jerome. Your father and Uncle were good men."

Jerome

"Thank you, Mr. Napels."

John Gotti

"Sorry, Jerome. If there is anything I can do for you, please let me know."

Jerome

"Thank you, John."

My girl and I are at a party. It's about 1 am, and we are driving and entering the highway, going about 60mph. The next thing I saw was a tractor-trailer with no lights on; I hit the brakes and slammed into the back of the trailer.

Jerome

"Are you ok? Oh my God, no, no, no. Stay with me, baby, please, please, don't do this to me, no, no, not now, please, no, no, somebody help."

And she died right there. Her parents blamed me, or so I felt. That is when I decided to go to my family's house in South Florida.

five

1985 Delray Beach, FL. At Warehouse Davanzo Inc. Wholesale Flower and Plant co.

I'M PREPARING two of my friends and employees, Ricky and Jonny, to make a trip to Colombia to pick up flowers and smuggle cocaine back to the U.S. While I prepare to make deliveries to my clients from a previous delivery. I don't usually make the deliveries anymore, but I had a girl in Baltimore who I wanted to see.

The first delivery is to a nightclub in Baltimore, MD: my bodyguard and I.

The associate/bodyguard pulled up to the rear entrance of the nightclub in a limo, and the bouncer at the door said,

Bouncer

"Hey, what's up, Romy, my brother?"

Jerome

"Cool, cool, my brother. Good to see you."

Entering through the kitchen and going up the stairs to the club office, knock on the door and enter.

JP

> "Hey, Romy, right on time."

Jerome

> "All good, all good."

JP

> "All right, good to hear."

We make a briefcase exchange, and I hand mine to my bodyguard.

Jerome

> "Ya know, I'd like to stay and party with you boys, but I'm a white man in a black man's world here; peace out, JP. Be good, see you in two weeks."

Back downstairs, I drive off to spend the rest of the evening with the girl I came to see.

On the freeway going north, a sign says 'New York City - 10 miles', and a car pulls up to a high-rise—apartment complex in the Bronx. Once again, we got out of the vehicle.

Black Boy

“You in the wrong neighborhood, white boy. Do you want to die?”

Bodyguard

“Don't you mind us, little boy?”

He shows the gun in the holster as we proceed to enter the building and take the elevator to the penthouse.

Black Boy

“Hey, hey, what's up?”

Bodyguard

"Hold on, bro, I’ll be right with you.”

Black Boy

“No problem, bro.”

Sitting down on the couch.

Dealer two

“Make yourself a cocktail, Romy.

My guard goes to the bar and makes cocktails. Dealer Two comes out of the room; two girls follow.

Dealer two

“Yoyo, what’s up, bro?

Jerome

“Same old, same old. You know what time it is.”

Dealer two

“Hey, babe, take that briefcase into my room, get the one out of my safe, and bring it to me.”

He takes the cocktail off the bar and has a bathrobe sitting down in the living room.

Girl one

“Shit, what do I look like, your nigger bitch?”

Dealer two

"Shut up bitch. Do what I say.”

Girl one goes and gets the briefcase and brings it out to me. I give it to my bodyguard.

Girl two

"Damm"

She snorts a line off the table and picks her head up.

six

In 1985, Steve Heller gets arrested at an Iranian airport with a suitcase full of hashish.

Customs

"HEY, you, yes you, come with me."

(SCREEN NOT FINISHED)

Steve gets arrested and is imprisoned in an Iranian prison.

Boynton Beach, FL. My home is on the Intracoastal. My brother, Anthony, is there, and he is a priest. We go into my office, where we make confessions.

Jerome

"Bless me, Father, for I have sinned."

Anthony

"Yes, my brother."

Jerome

"Well, I've killed several (shrugging shoulders), okay, many bad men. I'm a drug dealer, and I have prostitutes several nights a week, just to say the least."

Anthony

"I know what you do. We're brothers. Say 10 Hail Marys and 10 Our Fathers."

Jerome

"Thank you, Father, brother. (whisper to self) That's fucked up."

At Warehouse Davanzo Inc.

So my father taught me a lot about business as I grew up, teaching me about family business. Now, it was my turn. The family businesses pretty much ran themselves at this point; I had the staff to do so.

I'm 20 years old, and this is how I met Richard.

Richard owned a 10-acre lot of land. I had heard from a friend that he had offered him an opportunity to start a tree nursery on the land, and he turned it down, so I immediately jumped on the opportunity. So he had the land cleared, laid down the ground cover, and put in a well and pump, sprinkler system and propagation house, which I hired and supervised the contractors to do so. This is where I got my land clearing and contracting experience from. (which I'll talk about later.) Then I sent a laborer out with a truck to collect seeds and cuttings off job sites, which they were glad to give me because it was their garbage. I had a girl at the nursery that would plant the cuttings and seeds in the greenhouse.

So, as you can see, this type of business takes time to build. The cuttings and seeds for the bushes took 6 months to grow, and the trees would take several years. That's how I had time to take care of my personal and illegal businesses. I sold the bushes when they were ready—but still had to wait on the trees. Now, at this point, I created a landscaping division and was installing my nursery stock. I could beat anybody's price because the material I was installing grew from seeds and cuttings. Growing plants was like a small commodity market. You never knew what other growers in the area were going to grow, so if you grew something nobody else grew, you could get a pretty penny for it.

This is where I began learning economics. Do you see how everything just falls into place for me? So, a couple of years later, I created a tree trimming and removal company. You're going to like this. Now I'm growing, installing and cutting down the trees I grew from seeds, only to replace them with other trees I grow. And it gets better; believe it or not, some of the trees I was contracted to remove, I would dig, bring back to the farm and sell them again. I sold trees back to the same communities that paid me to take them out. Next, I started a land clearing division. I bought a wood chipper to grind all the trees up and turn them into mulch and topsoil, of course, using the topsoil in my plant nursery and selling the mulch. I had literally no overhead except for my crews doing all the labor.

Now, I think this next part was in God's hands. I'm driving down the Frontage road along the railroad track, and my truck breaks down; up walks a homeless man and points to the debris I have in the back of my truck and says,

Homeless

"Hey, you know they use that wood to make silk trees. They drill holes in it and attach silk leaves and frons to them."

He helped me fix the truck, and I took him out to lunch, gave him my business card and told him to call me in a few weeks. I contacted some wholesale silk tree manufacturers and started selling the wood. Mind you, this is my garbage. I owned several tractor-trailers from the tree company and started delivering the wood. For some of the palm stalks, I got 3x the price for the wood as I got for taking out the tree I was paid to remove. Yes, pretty soon, I was selling the wood all over the country. Everything I did was just pure profit.

Back at my office, a homeless man called me back. I set him up with an apartment, a job, and an F150 pickup truck.

Richard

"Hi Jerome"

Jeorme

“Hey, Richard,”

Richard

“How have you been?”

Jerome

"Good, good. What can I do for you?”

Richard

“I've got a little problem and need your help again.”

Jerome

“Okay, what's up?”

Richard

“One of my guys got busted in Iran for bringing out a suitcase of hashish. As you know, the Iranian government will absolutely not deal with the Jewish mafia, so I proposed to hire you for the job to negotiate the release of my guy.”

Jerome

“Let me see what I can do; I'll get back to you.”

Richard

"Okay. "

(Standing up, shaking hands.)

One-week later. The phone rings. I pick it up.

Jerome

"Davanzo Inc., this is Jerome. How may I help you? Oh, hi Richard."

Richard

"We have some commodities coming in tonight. How would you like to come out with us tonight?"

Jerome

"Sure, when and where?"

Richard

"Sebastian Inlet, 4:00"

Jerome

"Okay, Rich, see you there."

Richard

"Don't forget your fishing pole" (laughing)

Richard, his two goons and I were on a cigarette boat in the Atlantic Ocean.

Richard

"So Jerome, this is how we do it."

(Goon #1 gets missile launcher out of boat floorboard)

"You see the weather balloon up there."

(hands me binoculars)

"That's the radar system to indicate what boats are in the ocean; there is another one in Key West that's their way of tracking the smugglers in and out of South Florida; we're about to take it out with Rocket and shut down the system for about a week so our goods can come and go undetected."

Jerome

"Rich, where did you get that rocket?"

Richard

“Well, Jerome, I'm not only the largest chain of floral shops in the Northeast; I'm also an international weapons dealer.”

Jerome

"No shit, that's awesome. That's why Steve is over there in Iran. It makes sense now; I’m putting together a plan to get Steve out. I've already contacted my people in Iran.”

Richard

"Marking target"

Jerome

“Target is hot. Fire when ready.

(whoosh boom)

Goon one

“Target hit!”

(Everybody is clapping; cheering turns to laughter.)

Richard

“Boats can come and go at will now.”

We go to a safe house and wait for the boats to come to the Intracoastal home and unload.

Back to Colombia, loading the plane with cocaine and flowers.

(A bunch of Spanish lingo.)

Jerome

> "You know, Escobar, I will give you a little advice: you need to get in and get out, make the money and run; otherwise, you wind up dead or in prison."

Rick Funk is a Miami police officer. We grew up together; I met him in the first grade. He is my best friend; he also works for me and several of his friends from the department. But Ricky runs the crew. He is one of my brothers. I love Ricky.

Rick

> "The plane is loaded and ready for takeoff."

Jerome

> "Okay, boys, have a safe trip. See you in the States."

Jonny

> "No problem, we've got this, bro." (laughing)

Rick

"Fuck you, Jonny, get in the fucking plane, you goof-ball. This is real shit. Not everything's funny."

(Jonny flips Rick off)

The plane is flying back to the States. Jonny turns on the radio. 'great song.' Then the engine fails; the plane is drifting.

Rick

"Oh, shit, we lost the engine, Jonny."

Jonny

"Ahh, Fuck me, do something, do something, Rick."

Rick

"Damn it, damn it, Jonny, I'm fucking trying, Jonny, shut up."

Jonny

"We're going to die, Ricky."

Rick

"Hold on, Jonny, we're going to make a crash landing."

Jonny

"Hail Mary, full of grace, the Lord is with you."

The plane hits the water and breaks apart; everything sinks slowly. The only things left are a few bales of cocaine and roses floating.

Funeral of Rick and Jonny

Jerome

"Good morning, everybody. It takes my breath away to see so many people here, but I know why you are here. We loved Rick Funk and John Day; I can hear them now laughing and arguing in heaven, both smiling. We didn't give Rick the nickname smiley for nothing, so at this celebration of life for Rick Funk and John Day, we should all be smiling for the gift of life they both shared with us. Don't you think that's what they would want? I see this tragedy as now I shall have two more guardian angels on my shoulders; although they were too young to pass, it wasn't our choice. Evidently, God needed their help and called upon them as two angels to guide the living. I can feel their presence among us right now. I can feel their joyful spirits among us now; for one moment, they suffered, died and were buried and rose again in fulfillment of the scriptures and are seated at the right hand of our Father, so I bow my head and say, 'God thank you for so many gifts. Thank you for the time you let me share in life with Rick and John, my two most loyal brothers.'

I turn around and face Jesus, get on my knees, and say:

"Jesus, please give us the strength to move on and stop the pain we feel for our loss of these two heavenly angels that touched so many lives, in the name of the Father, the Son, and the Holy Spirit, amen."

There was a full police escort to the cemetery. So they were buried at sea, and both the coffins had some of their personal belongings. Their bodies were never recovered.

After the funeral, my attorney is on a plane flying back from Minnesota to South Florida.

Jerome

"Shit, you know I just lost my two best guys."

Craig Flick

"Yeah, I know, they were my friends too. I've known Jonny since the 1st grade."

Jerome

"Yeah, just like me and Ricky, we have been friends since the first grade; he was like a brother to me, fucking sad, fuck, fuck, all my fault."

Craig

"Don't even go there. Fuck you" (shaking head)

Jerome

"This is why I pay cash up front: no boss, no one to answer to. Imagine if I lost 20 kilos of Pablo's cocaine; he would kill me right on the spot. I make my own rules, you know. It seems like every time things are going well for me, something kicks me, something kicks me in the balls, so here is what I've been thinking: you were the smartest kid in our group of friends; that's why my father paid for your law school, and I think it's time for you to come on full-time. You know my right-hand man; you know you have to pay the favor back. And I'm pulling my card. You know how much money I have; you know better than I do that I have it spread out all over the world in offshore accounts."

Craig

"60,000,000 dollars, give or take a few."

Jerome

"Whatever, there is plenty enough for me to pay you more than you'll ever make anywhere else."

Craig

"True, true"

Jerome

"You're my best friend, so give it some consideration, to say the least."

Craig

"So, not to change the subject, I think this is the right time to bring this up. You keep putting aside your living will."

Jerome

"Well, it's just going to be split up by my family, and that's just what happens. It's the way it works; I don't need to put it on paper."

Craig

"Well, you see what can happen. God can pull your number at any time. Your job is very dangerous; besides, you could have a heart attack, an accident, or, who knows, get 'whacked.'"

Jerome

"Ok, ok, we'll get it done; you will get 15%. You can build a hospital in a 3rd world country, then split the rest up with my family."

Craig

"$60,000,000, plus whatever you make from here on out."

Jerome

“I pay $7,000 per kilo, and I get $27,000 here in the U.S. That's a profit of $20,000. Per kilo, that's a lot of money.”

At the hotel, I am with my mistress. We are getting ready to go to a party at Pablo Escobar’s home.

Jerome

“Ahhh, an American! How are you doing? (shaking hands) Jerome Davanzo.”

Barry Seals

“Barry Seal, nice to meet you. How do you know Pablo?”

Jerome

"He’s been a friend of the family for a long time, and he and my uncle George Jung did a lot of business in the 1970s.”

(clip in a scene from Jonny, deep BLOW)

Barry Seals

"Do you work for Pablo?”

Jerome

“No, do you know who I am?

Bary Seals

"No"

Jerome

"I'm one of the most connected men in the world. Pablo is a client of mine; my father is Carmine Davanzo."

Barry seals.

"Oh shit"

Jerome

"My family handled the Cuban Missile Crisis in the '60s and the New York dock problem for the government. Sometimes, the government has hired my family to take care of world issues."

Back to my home in South Florida. A black escalade pulls up to my mailbox and inserts a folder. I retrieve my mail and go back into my house. I open the folder, and it reads the FBI is about to indict me on international drug trafficking. It reads we should meet at the Boynton Beach mall in front of Macey's tomorrow at noon. Look for a black Mercedes.

(Insert news clip of Tom Brokaw reporting on the assignment of Barry Seals)

NEWS

"He used to Smuggle drugs and got caught. He became the government's most valuable informant—war on cocaine, but last night in Louisiana, Barry Seal's enemies caught up with him and killed him.

Tonight, three men are in custody. NBC's Brian Roths reports that Seals was about to Testify for the government.

Authorities believe last night's machine-gun killing of top Government informant Barry Seals was ordered by top drug bosses in Medellin, Colombia.

Who sent five men to baton rouge to kill, Seal's son Barry JR. was restrained by police, who said the gunmen had waited in ambush at the Salvation Army where Seal had been sentenced on a drug charge to do community service."

seven

1986. At Boynton Beach Mall

12:00, Mercedes pulls up to me.

(Show Regan's address to the nation on Iran contra)

My fellow Americans, I've spoken to you from this historical office on many occasions and about many things. The power of the presidency is often thought to reside within this Oval Office, yet it doesn't rest here. It rests in you, the American people and in your trust. Your trust is what gives a president his power of leadership and his personal strength, and it's what I want to talk to you about this evening. For the past three months, I've been silent about the revolutions in Iran, and you must have been thinking, why doesn't he tell us what's happening? Why doesn't he just speak to us as he has in the past when we face troubles and tragedies? Other of you, I guess, were thinking, what is he doing hiding out in the White House? Well, the reason I haven't spoken to you before now is this: you deserve the truth and as frustrating as the wait has been, I felt it was improper to come to you with sketchy reports or possibly even erroneous statements which would then have to be corrected creating more doubt and confusion. There's been enough of that I've paid the price for my silence in terms of your trust and confidence. Still, I've had to wait as you have for the complete story. That is why I've appointed Ambassador David Abshire as my special counselor to help get out the thousands of documents to the various investigations and appointed a special review board, the Tower board, which took on the core of pulling the truth together for me and getting to the bottom of things.

I have now issued its findings, which state that I am often accused of being an optimist. It is true l head hunt pretty hard to find any goods in the board report, as you know, it's well stalked with criticisms which I'll discuss in a moment, but I was very relieved to read this sentence 'The board is convinced that the President does indeed want the full story to be told' and that will continue to be my pledge to you as the other investigations go forward, I want to thank the members of the panel, former senator John Tower former secretary of state Edmond Musky and former national security advisor Brent Scowcroft they have done the nation as well as me personally by submitting a report of such integrity and depth they have my genuine and gratitude. I've studied the board's report.

Its studies are honest, convincing, and highly critical, and I accept tonight I want to share with you my thoughts on these findings and report on the actions I am taking to implement the board implications. First, let me say I take full responsibility for my own actions and that of my administration. As angry as I may be about the activities undertaken without my knowledge, I am still accountable for those activities.

As disappointed as I may be in some who have served me. I am the one who must still answer to the American people, and as personally disgraceful as I find secret bank accounts and diverted funds, as the navy would say, this happened on my watch. Let's start with the most controversial part: a few months ago, I told the American people I did not trade arms for hostages.

My heart and my best intentions still tell me that's true, but the facts and evidence tell me it is not; as the Tower board reported what began a strategic opening to Iran, I disagreed with its implementation into traded arms for hostages. This runs counter to my own beliefs about administrative policy, and under the original strategy we had in mind, there are reasons why it happened, but no excuses. 'It was a mistake. I undertook the original Iran initiative in order to develop relations with those who might assume leadership in a post-Homani government. It's clear from the board's report, however, that I let my personal concern for the hostages spill over into the GO political strategy of reaching out to Iran. I asked so many questions about the hostages. We'll say that I didn't ask enough about the specifics of the total Iran plan.

Let me say to the hostage's families we have not given up, we never will, and I promise you a legitimate way to free your loved ones from captivity. There's one more thing upsetting me, which, however, is that no one kept proper records of meetings or decisions.

(Show Oliver North shredding documents)

This led to my failure to recollect whether I approved an arms shipment before or after the fact; I did approve it, I just can't say specifically when. But rest assured, there's plenty of record-keeping going on now at 1600 Pennsylvania Ave. For nearly a week now, I've been studying the board's report. I want the American people to know that this reaching ordeal of recent months has not been in vain. I endorse every one of the Tower board's recommendations so as to put the house in better order. I am taking action in three basic areas: personnel, National Security policy, and the process of making sure that the system works. First, personally, I brought in an accomplished and highly respected new team here at the White House. They bring new blood, new energy and new credibility and experience. Former Senator Howard Baker is my new chief of staff.

In the area of national security policy, I have ordered the NSC to begin a comprehensive of all covert operations. I have also directed that any covert activity is in support of clear policy objectives and compliance with American morals and values. I expect a covert policy that, if Americans saw it on the front page of the newspaper, would say that makes sense. I have issued a directive prohibiting the NSC staff itself from undertaking covert operations, no ifs or buts. My fellow Americans, Thank you, Goodnight, and god bless.

Oliver North

"Hello, Mr. Davanzo. **M**y name is Oliver North, and my partner's name is Agent Shaffer; we need your help. Can you get in the vehicle with us and take a short ride?"

Jerome

"Absolutely"

Oliver

"We are prepared to give you full amnesty, he said, holding my FBI file and waiving it at me. We need your help with your people in South America. This is a highly classified CIA op, and we know how you operate in secrecy. We're fighting a war in Nicaragua, and Congress cut our funding (the Boland Act). We need your help getting cocaine smuggled into the U.S., and you will be compensated for it."

Jerome

"I think I can help you. I'm going to give you an account number in the Caymans to deposit funds into."

I write the number on a piece of paper and hand it to Oliver.

Jerome

"Come back in a week, and I will give you a key to a storage unit."

The drugs were coming from everywhere: Bolivia, Peru, Columbia, Honduras, and Panama. Almost all of South America was corrupt, and the same with the weapon dealers: Russia, Pakistan, Israel, Iran, and Iraq. Everything was so globalized nobody really knew or trusted anybody. Times were crazy; everyone was making a lot of money. Things just snowballed; I went from smuggling cocaine to being a weapons contractor. Not to mention George Bush's deregulation of the savings and loan industry in 1986, free money, hundreds of millions of dollars to finance drug and weapon deals and the filling of bankruptcies with Boynton beaches.

The headquarters for Sunshine Savings and Loan is located in Boynton Beach, leaving taxpayers with half a trillion dollars in debt. We all had get-out-of-jail-free cards because of our involvement with the CIA.

So now I have been assigned a partner, and we have become very close, the kind of bond two soldiers on a battlefield would have. Marc is a single parent and has a daughter, and he tells me to promise him that if anything ever happens to him, I will see to it that his daughter is taken care of. Well, wouldn't you know it? Marc gets killed in a boating accident shortly after, and I adopt his daughter. So, I do as I promised and teach her the ropes. I send her to all the best schools around the world. She comes home for summer break and all the holidays. I will send her to learn karate while she is home.

Now we were in Nicaragua supporting the contras, trying to oust the communist Sandinistas.

(Show war scene: shit blowing up, moving weapons, unloading trucks in the jungle).

Jerome

"Hey, soldier, get over here and get this truck unloaded. This war is a monster."

Soldier one

"Well, normal people don't become good soldiers; only the fearless."

Jerome

"The only time killing is justified is in times of war, but don't you think there are bad people who deserve to die? It's war: good vs. evil; therefore, justified. But no man deserves to die if he is fighting for what he believes in."

"You can smell it, Death; it hurts your nose."

Soldier two

"You can't be sane to stay alive here; nothing makes sense here."

Jerome

"WOW, this is hell, nothing but hate, evil, and fear."

Soldier one

"Your probability of getting out of here alive is about 20%."

Now we are going up a Harry Carry mountain road, and we get stopped by armed soldiers pointing AK47s at us; they check us out, and we proceed to the next drop point.

We proceeded to get the truck unloaded and get on the plane that was waiting for us, Global International Airlines, which was based out of Kansas City on a loan from the savings and loan, and headed to Iran to get more weapons.

(Richard is supplying the weapons out of Isreal)

The plane lands in Iran. We unload suitcases of money we have from the cocaine dealings into the trunk of the Mercedes. We take off and go into the city, where we meet with a CIA operative. We were taken to a safe house and unloaded the suitcases to the agents to buy weapons to go back to the contras. I slip away from the party and go to a hotel room with two smaller briefcases. I couldn't tell anybody about my meeting with Shaw; he was a target, but he was also one of my intel connections in the Middle East. I was the only American agent who could get close enough to take him out; I figured since he had cancer and was going to die anyway, I was gaining a relationship with Steve Heller, who was intelligence for Israel.

At this time, the agents at the safe house where we made the large money drop are noticing that their money is $13,000,000 short.

Agent one

"That little S.O.B. was $13,000,000 short; there's $15.5 million here."

Agent two

"He tricked us; he's got some business going on over here, and he just got off with some of our money."

Agent one

"That little fucker stole our money, and there's nothing we can do about it."

Agent 2

"He knew he could get away with it because this was all classified National Security shit."

I'm now in a hotel room on the phone, setting up a meeting to get Steve Heller out of an Iranian prison.

Jerome

"Ya hey, it's Jerome ready to get Steve."
"Yes, I'll send you the info."

I'm in a hotel room, unpacking and looking at my watch. I go downstairs, where a taxi driver is waiting for me.

Jerome

"Take me to the Marriott Palace."

Taxi Driver

"Yes, sir."

At the Marriott, I go up to the front desk.

Jerome

"Davanzo"

Clerk

"Here you go. Enjoy your stay, Mr. Davanzo."

Jerome

"Thank you"

I go to the room and wait. The phone rings. I pick it up.

Jerome

"Ok"

I go down the elevator, where there are two men in military uniforms on each side of the elevator. They whisk me out of the building, where there are two SUVs, two Mercedes, and two jeeps with mounted machine guns as we go flying through town toward the airport.

Kadifi

"How are you doing, Mr. Jerome?"

Jerome

"Hi, Kadaifi, (shaking hands) I have $10,000,000 I stole from the CIA. Please put this to build a hospital for the people. Do you have Steve?"

Kadaifi

"Yes, Mr. Jerome, in the car in front of us."

Jerome

"Thank you, Kadaifi."

Getting dropped off at the airport, Steve and Kadaifi go through customs, get on a private jet, and fly back to Miami International Airport.

Steve

"What took you so long?

Jerome

"Richard hired me to get you out of here, and it's not that easy. You have no idea what I went through to get here, Steve."

"Cocktails? Your government is to be gratefully in debt to me for getting one of their top ops out of there with discretion."

Steve

"Well, anyway, thank you for everything. It's great to be out of that hellhole."

The plane lands at Miami Airport, and as I am leaving the airport, my cell phone rings.

Jerome

"Hi, this is Jerome."

John Gotti

"Hi, Jerome, this is John Gotti."

Jerome

"How are you, sir?"

John Gotti

"Good, but I need your help. Things are in a bit of a crisis right now, and your family has always been the ones to call to handle these types of situations. We're having a bloodbath here, and it's not good for anyone.

Jerome

"Yes, sir. See you in a couple of days."

Home of John Gotti, NY, NY.

John

"Hi, Jerome, come in. How have you been?"

Jerome

"Good, good, John. It's been a while. How the hell are you doing."

We go to Johns's office and sit down.

"First thing I want to know is who killed my father: was it Castellano?"

John

"Yes, Jerome, I knew you'd be coming."

Jerome

"Okay, thanks for killing that fucking bastard, but that's not enough. I need to know who pulled the trigger."

John Gotti

"Jerome, you were just about to be a made man; as a matter of fact, the youngest ever. We were going to finish that, and you would have had full power to clean this mess up."

John writes a name on a piece of paper and hands it to me.

Jerome

"Okay, John, I'll be back after I take care of a little business."

John Gotti

"Okay, Jerome, thanks for coming."

eight

1991 Youngstown, Ohio home of Joey Naples

I'M SITTING in the cornfield across the street with an M14; Naples pulls up, gets out of the car, walks up to the front door and pop, pop, pop, target has gone.

"That's one 's' for you pops."

(Show the newscast of Joey Naples's death)

News caster

"On the evening of August 12th, 1991, well-known Mahoning Vally Mafia figure, Joseph N "little Joey Naples Jr. " was gunned down while he was checking out the house he was having built in Beaver Township, the murder has not been solved."

Back in South Florida. I ran an ad in the newspaper for a live-in maid cook and hired a girl named Lisa; a couple of days later, we very quickly fell in love. I have my cousin Ricky and his wife coming down from Youngstown for a week's vacation, and Lisa told me.

Lisa

"They can have your bedroom, and you can sleep with me in mine."

Back in Delray Beach.FL., at my house with my Fiance, she is drinking and snorting cocaine AM-PM every day, and I'm getting tired of it.

Jerome

"How are you going to be the mother of my children if you're going to be all fucked up all the time?"

Lisa

"Fuck you, I'll just kill myself."

Jerome

"Don't talk like that. Let's get you to a doctor and get you some help."

nine

In 1990

I GOT HIRED ONCE AGAIN by the CIA to assassinate Communist Party members who were disrupting our government. I also got married and had a big Italian wedding. The marriage ended in 11 months with a divorce after I found out she was having an affair because I was never there, as she didn't think I would find out. I had eyes all over the world, but how could she have known? She had no idea who I really was. She thought I owned a flower shop and I couldn't kill her; it was too close to home. 6 months later, she was diagnosed with ovarian cancer and passed two months later.

(Go to funeral)

So, at this time, I'm a very powerful man. My brother works for the University of Florida in Gainsville, and he is in charge of inspecting all the land that was going to be built on otherwise construction projects. The University provided him with an airplane, helicopter and a pilot, and he had a direct line to Governor Jeb Bush. Now, I was a consultant to a man named George May, which was not his real name, by the way. He was a third-generation real estate mogul in South Florida and worked closely with President George Bush, so if there were any issues or red tape, I would just call my brother and inform him what sites were ours. He could just pass our properties to have the go-ahead to build on. In reality, I controlled all the development in Florida.

My next mission was to get Jeb Bush re-elected as the Govener. So what I did next was write an article for the newspapers to run on the front page. I paid for this; it was like a paid advertisement, but I designed it to look like real news; it was a little controversial, and I manipulated the population to sway Jeb Bush into re-election, and of course, it worked, he shot right up in the polls and took the election. So now I control the government and all the development in the state of Florida. Wow, what the fuck, it was just a game to me.

So, I'm in a meeting with the biggest builders in the world, and we are working on a 300,000,000-dollar project for which I was the head of real estate and finance.

We owned the last undeveloped I-95 interstate quadrant. From Miami to New York City, we purchased it on a bank loan, so we actually leveraged the property with a down payment. It was pretty ingenious how we did that; everybody wanted a piece of the action.

So anyways! Just single-handedly got the governor re-elected, and during the meeting,

Boss

"I bet Jerome had something to do with this."

I reach into my briefcase, pull out copies of the article, and pass them out to everyone in the meeting; they all laugh.

All

"The kid's a fucking genius."

So now I've done a few things that may be considered in the grey area, and the Florida Real Estate Commission put up charges against me. So the agent comes down from the capitol in Tallahassee and comes into our set appointment at my attornies office. He took some paperwork out of his briefcase, put it on the table,

Jerome

"Do you know who I am? I am a consultant to George May,"

Boss

"George May, oh,"

As he was packing up his briefcase.

"We don't prosecute anybody that works for your group."

He closes his briefcase and apologizes as he leaves the office.

Shortly after, I received a letter from the Governor linking me and stating that they were closing the investigation and would never be discussed again. So, during all this, I went to college and spent 9 years doing so to achieve four degrees: one in Real Estate, one in finance, one in economics and one in business.

I speak eight languages: English, French, Arabic, Spanish, Russian, Chinese and Italian. Which really helped me out with my world travels and assignments, if you know what I mean. I also opened up a property mgmt. Company and maintenance company in Boca Raton, FL., which has the most prestigious H.O.A.s in the entire country.

They were required by law to get three estimates on all the work done on their properties, which were contracts from $80.000 to $1,000,000 per year. I got about 85% of them in Palm Beach County. How I did that was to create three dummy corporations along with my real corporation. I ran four advertisements in the Yellow Pages, each a 1\4 of a page, so when the H.O.A.s called for their required three estimates, they called all my numbers; this way, I ousted the competition, and I gave them three highly inflated estimates. I thought to myself, 'Is it really this easy? is everyone on this planet that stupid?' I had 1000 employees working for me, and I just had to collect checks.

Don't get me wrong, I did have to start the companies and hire the staff to run them, and of course, my managers and sales staff were told to let me know when we worked on private properties to inform of any famous people so I could be on the job site to meet the people to broaden my connections by befriending them, that is how I met Donald and Marla Trump, Rod Stewert just to name a couple.

I had my hands on a little of everything, and my friends said that whatever I touched turned to gold. I'm starting to drift a little here, so let's go back to my story about the Florida Real Estate Commission.

What did I do? Well, one of the things was that I sold 5-acre plots that were zoned to be 20-acre lots. I subdivided 200 acres into 40 5-acre lots, and the county tried to tell me that was illegal. They would not let the people who purchased the lots get permits to build there. Now, of course, I had 40 lawsuits against me, and they defaulted on their loans with me, and I resold all the land they had defaulted on their loan payments to me. So what did I do next? I resold all 40 lots again at $100,000 each, both times with a 50% down payment, which is low for land; the banks require a 70% down payment on the land and will only finance the remainder 30%. But I was being a nice guy and financing the properties at 6% interest. Now, the judge did throw me in jail for 1 night for contempt of court. I was out the next morning, and I continued to sell and re-sell the lots, many times, over and over; people should have trusted me.

McDonald's and several other corporations like Shell Gas also purchased lots next to mine; they taught me in school that the best marketing tools were fear and greed. Well, I guess I'm a pretty fast learner; all my sales were made on greed. It was the last undeveloped 1-95 quadrant in the country. So let me explain; I'm watching the president's address to the nation, speaking about the war in Iraq. Did he not say that Iraq must not violate the treaty we have with them on building, making and testing weapons of mass destruction? So, the rest of the world must not violate treaties.

Ok, I get it, so when I present the Jay Treaty of 1703, which treaties are above and beyond the Declaration of Independence of the United States of America that was signed in 1776. To the courts, it clearly states when we purchased most of the Southern

States of our great nation, including Florida, that the land is to be held by the owners, the people and may be used in any way desirable to them with the protection of the USA, meaning, they can sell 1 inch of there land if they desire. I reckon Smiths also make zoning policing and the entire court system illegal. I told the judge he was breaking the law just by sitting in that chair in front of me. Now I'm up against the court with no lawyer on the defense stand; my attorney, Craig, was sitting in the back row the whole time, enjoying this travesty more than I was; he actually told me after it was all said and done that I needed to fire him.

Craig

"You don't need a lawyer? You need a lobotomy."

We went back to my house, hit my bar, and laughed until we cried.

> "You should have seen the look on the judge's face when you quoted passages out of the Jay Treaty, and he knew you were right. His face almost blew off; it turned into every color of the spectrum, and then he almost tripped over his jaw when you approached the bench to give him a copy. I thought he was going to have a heart attack."

Laughing the whole time through his statement.

How can the President say to the nation that the treaty must be followed and disregard our treaties? Well, needless to say, I never spent another minute in jail or his courtroom. Oh yeah, and once again, I got the letter, but this time it wasn't from the governor; it was from the president, and in the letter, it stated

> *Mr.Davanzo, I have been briefed by the Central Intelligence Agency, and I don't know what you've done, but I understand that you've served this country well. Your point has been clearly made, and in the future, if you have anything you would like to discuss, here is my direct phone number and thanks again for your patriotism.*

Later, we went golfing together; he said I had a strange way of making friends, and what he heard was that I'm quite a brilliant man. I didn't have the heart to tell him I came from a sports family, and I've been golfing since I was knee-high to a grasshopper; my uncle Mike was a pro golfer in his youth. I just shanked a few and let him beat me. After all, he was the President.

ten

In 1990

CANADIAN WEAPONS DEALER Gerald Bull died in Brussels, Belgium, on March 22, two days after being shot several times near his apartment. The shooter has never been identified.

eleven

In 1991

THE BODY OF ROBERT DONATI, a Boston-area mobster, was found beaten and stabbed in the trunk of his car on September 24; no suspects have ever been charged.

twelve

In 1992

PIOTR JAROSZEWICZ, a former Prime Minister of communist Poland, was found murdered along with his wife, Aicija Solska, at their home in the Warsaw suburb. On September 3, he was strangled with a belt; no suspects have been named.

thirteen

In 1993

MODANI BHANDARI, the General Secretary of the Communist Party of Nepal, died in a car accident on May 16; it is suspected that it was a murder.

> "You wouldn't be safe anywhere if I had a contract on you. It was just a job, and I was good at it. The only evidence I left was the evidence of death."

(Go to newscast Pablo Escabar's Death)

> "Good evening. The king is dead. Pablo Escobar, the Colombian drug king who was for years one of the world's most wanted men, was gunned down today by the Colombian police in the Colombian city of Medellin. His drug cartel was named after the city that he had controlled for so long. He was only 44 years old, enough for cocaine to make him one of the world's richest men. He was rich and ruthless enough to have hundreds of people who got in his way killed, from people who ran drugs to people who ran the country. Here ABCs Mark Potter."

Police say Escobar was killed by a shopping mall in Medrian, Colombia. He was shot to death by members of an elite police squad that had been searching for him since he escaped from this prison outside Madrian about a year and a half ago. Colombia's prosecutor called Escobar's killing “excellent” for his country. U.S. drug agents said it was also good for the United States, where he faced numerous charges.

fourteen

In 1994

HEADLINES READ, "Driver kills man in Delray Beach in car crash." I'm all fucked up and go to the hospital, and I call Craig, who now lives in Boynton Beach

(Insert news cast police giving details of the fatal crash in Delray Beach)

News reporter

"That's right, Todd, they have just towed away the cars involved in this fatal crash; it happened right at this intersection, right behind me; they say a Lamborghini was speeding and smashed into a Buick enclave, killing the driver of that Buick, this is one of the strangest fatal accidents I have ever covered."

"Here's what happened: it was around 4:30 this afternoon; police tell us that the driver of this yellow Lamborghini turned off Atlantic Avenue going north on the Federal Hwy, and they say he was speeding with a yellow Porshe next to him. They say the Buick Enclave was heading west; it stopped at the stop sign correctly and proceeded into the intersection, where the Lamborghini tee-boned it, then the Lamborghini crashed into the curb, hitting two parked cars. In the meantime, the driver of that Porshe pulled around to a side street, parked the car and disappeared. Police said that the driver of the Porshe was the girlfriend of the driver of the Lamborghini. The man in the Buick was killed, the Lamborghini driver was seriously injured, and the driver of the Porsche has disappeared; this is what the policewoman had to say."

Officer

"Right now, she is just considered a witness to this crash; she wasn't involved in the collision. She just left the scene, and detectives really want to talk to her just to help us piece together what happened that led to this fatal crash."

News Reporter

"And police tell us they don't know why that female driver of the Porshe would have left her seriously injured boyfriend in the Lamborghini; he was taken to the hospital; we don't know his condition right at this moment. Employees at Coal Fire Pizza rushed out and tried to give the driver of the Buick CPR, but they were not successful, and he died at the hospital; neither has been identified, but a witness told me that the driver of the Lamborghini seemed to be a younger man, in his thirties, the driver of the Buick was an older gentleman. Police ask that if you saw this accident or know anything about the Lamborghini that was seen parked on Atlantic Avenue earlier this afternoon, please call the Delray Beach Police Dept. Live at Delray Beach, this is Terri Parker, reporting from WPTV news."

My panic button went off in my Lamborghini; they are installed in all my vehicles; it alerted all government departments, The CIA, FBI, ATF, and DEA. I'm talking to a woman's voice.

Jerome

"Agent down! Agent down!"

Woman's Voice

"Okay, Jerome, we will have someone on the scene in minutes."

Jerome

"Okay, just get the girl. Palie, stand down, stand down."

Agent one

"Get in the SUV! Get in the SUV now!"

She is guided into the SUV and placed in the back by Agent One.

Agent one

"Have you been drinking?"

Agent two

“Yes, who are you?”

Agent two

“Federal agents (flashes badge) ‘we’re here to help you’”

Girl

“What?” (confused)

Agent two

"Well, let your boyfriend explain; right now, we’re taking you to Jerome’s home.”

The swooping up of my girl by the Feds makes Lori a bit nervous. The agents tell her,

FED

“Don't answer the phone. Don't answer the door. Don't speak to anyone about this incident. Wait here (at my home) until we get this straightened out; we'll be back.”

She didn't have a clue what had just happened. Do I tell her I work for the President? I’m kinda like a sniper, but I have to get a little closer to the target. No, she is freaking out, and I’m just going to have to break up with her. The accident puts me in the spotlight, so now I’m going to have to stay low for a while.

They transferred me as soon as I was in stable condition. I wasn't sure if I even existed anymore.

My home Delray Beach.

Lori

"What the hell was that Jerome"

Jerome

"I'm sorry, I don't know what to tell you. I work for the government, and I do the dirty work."

Lori

"Yes, it all makes sense now, all the little stuff, and when I put it together, I see I'm interchanged, but I can't be with you."

Jerome

"Well, nobody can. I can't even be with myself. You're the only one I've ever told that to, and it puts you in a dangerous place, but I wasn't going to lie to you. Do not ever repeat what I told you; if my cover is ever known, you will be at risk; you're going to be watched for a while now, so don't do anything stupid."

I start drinking at bars down on Atlantic Ave.

I haven't seen Lori for a while. In the meantime, the feds have Lori's fingerprints and DNA, and they can't find any information about her. That throws up a red flag; the only thing they have is that she is of Russian descendence from the DNA test. They put a lock on her car and started surveillance on her. She goes back to Russia, and the feds find out she is a spy. She knows everything about me; I've been played. When she is in Russia, she goes to her boss, and they tell her.

Boss

"You have to go back and keep him under surveillance. We do not want him in our country. If he is here, we know what he is here for."

Lori returns to the U.S.

Lori came back to my home out west in Delray Beach, and I was happy to see her; she came into my house, and we both started ripping each other's clothing off and fuck, and she went home the next day she called me and says,

Lori

"I miss you. Can I come over?"

Jerome

"Yes."

I poisoned her, put her dead body in the freezer and called my people for cleanup.

When I poisoned her, she was sitting across the table from me, looking right at me, and her vision started to blur; she stood up, knocking her chair over, and her knees buckled, and she dropped to the floor.

Jerome

"I'm sorry, babe, it was either you or me. I'll try to make this quick for you; I got on the floor, picked up her neck, and snapped it. It was quick."

After my clean-up was over, I got a call to report to Washington immediately. I got reamed for killing a Russian spy, especially on US soil, at home, but after I explained what had happened, it was considered a justified kill; my life was in jeopardy as my identity was breached.

Of course, I had a full-time private security team working for me. They were always in my shadow; they were all special ops, and they had my back 24/7.

Someone is trying to target me, and my bodyguard misses it, but my shadow takes him out. It happened at my business, Davanzo Inc. Paulie saved my life afterward.

Jerome

"Thank you, Pauile "

Paulie

"That's what you pay us for, boss."

Miami, FL. I'm on my way to court for my accident, driving a red Ferrari.

At the courthouse, we have to go through security and check our weapons. I show my badge and hand them my 38 semi-automatic. Gunner approaches security and surrenders his weapons; he has two 38s in shoulder straps, two strapped on his waist, and one strapped around his left ankle, and he takes off his bulletproof vest.

Attendant

"Damm"

(Show court scene: Craig is my lawyer and gets me off on medical issues.)

Jury

"The grounds of vehicular manslaughter, we, the jury, find the defendant not guilty."

The jury and judge were tainted by the CIA.

fifteen

In 1996

BACK IN IRAN, I'm inside the home of Cyrus Hasemi, waiting for the target. I go to the refrigerator, take out a beer, open it, sit in the living room, and wait. Next day headlines read:

> *Cyrus Hasemi, an Irani arm dealer, died suddenly on July 21. He was said to have contracted a rare form of leukemia, with which he was diagnosed two days earlier.*

A Draft House Committee reports the apparent suicide of Joeseph Danial Casolaro, a reporter found dead in his hotel room on August 31 with his wrists slashed. He was just two days from finishing his report on the Iran contra. There are suspicious circumstances surrounding his death.

My home Delray Beach, FL. I go to my safe and take out a bag. Now I'm in the bathroom tying a band around my arm and proceed to cook and shoot up some heroin after I pass out (the needle is still hanging out of my arm). I'm doing heroin now to get past the pain I have from the accident. I got it while I was in Afghanistan. It was pure. Craig is calling and calling, no answer; he comes over and finds me passed out on the bathroom floor. He calls 911, and the paramedics come and take me to the hospital, where the doctor sticks me with a shot, and I jump up and say.

"Shit, what happened?"

A few weeks later, I'm partying at my house with my prostitute her name is Shanna, and I have a heart attack. She calls 911, and I'm rushed to the hospital, where I have a triple bypass.

> "I'm in the back of the ambulance, and they hit me with the paddles. I jump up and shout out."

"What the fuck happened?

Paramedic

> "Cool down, bro, you're ok. You had a heart attack. You were flatlining for about 5 minutes. We got ya. Were you using any drugs?"

Jerome

"Heiorin and cocaine."

Paramedic

"That explains it."

There was a woman at the hospital before we even arrived. A C.I.A. agent heard my name over the air and took care of everything; she explained that I was one of theirs and there would be no paperwork necessary.

Womam

“He is a very high-level op; this is a hush-hush situation. We can’t blow his cover.”

Dr

"His cover keeps it up, and he's going to come in D.O.A.”

Woman

“Yes, sir, I'm going to recommend he enters a treatment program as soon as he gets out of here. Sometimes, our agents get in too deep to protect people like you and your family.”

Dr.

“Okay, ma'am, I don't want to see him here again. I'm a doctor, not a government agent. Next time, I won't let this go. Do you understand?”

Woman

“Yes, sir, thank you. Sorry, he’s just one of our best.”

Dr.

"Doesn't look like that to me. We're going to have to keep him for about a week; our tests are showing 90% blockage in his arteries. The surgeon is on his way."

Woman

"Okay, I'm staying also."

As she puts her hand down on her weapon, the Dr. leaves the room.

Woman

"What the fuck, Jerome, you asshole?"

Jerome

"You're wrong; I am the best."

Woman

"Fuck you"

Jerome

"Tell Gunnar to go home."

The following week, after I got out, my maid found me passed out on the kitchen floor and couldn't wake me. She calls 911, cleans up the paraphernalia, and off to the hospital, I go again. I was fucking her too.

I realized I couldn't sit and dwell and shoot heroin because I killed one man in a car accident. I'll just give the family $10,000,000.

sixteen
In 1998

TWO YEARS LATER, I'm walking out of rehab; everybody there sees me off and is shaking my hand, "Good luck." My attorney and best friend, Craig, pulls up in his Rolls Royce. Craig, that was the hardest fucking thing I've ever done in my whole life. I was clean now and ready to get back in the game again.

Pablo Escobar was dead, and John Gotti was in prison. All I had now was the C.I.A. So, I decided to do some local cleaning. Man shot to death inside a parked car in Boynton Beach.

(Show news clip)

We have a special unit: a man was shot and killed outside a church in Delray Beach.

(Show news clip.)

The two men were my local distributors of cocaine; they were putting 20 kilos per week on the streets. I'm starting to get noticed in the intelligence field, and it is time to slow down a bit and bam!

Sep 11, 911. It was a setup; they knew it was coming. Why would Jeb Bush, who owned the largest construction company in the state of Florida, suddenly shut down? Because he was preparing to move his company to Iraq to rebuild the country after we destroyed it, there would be billions of dollars in contracts, and his brother George was the President of the United States of America; intelligence knew the planes were coming, why do you think he was in Florida?

Jerome

"Oh, and by the way, my net worth was now well over $180,000,000."

Now, I like to have a little fun like everybody else. I have level 5 top secret clearance, so I go down to the Homestead Miami Air Force Base. They are doing a space shuttle launch tonight at Cape Canaveral, and all the air space in South Florida has become restricted air space. I get to go up in a f16. We are scraping the earth's atmosphere, and here comes the space shuttle; this is by far the coolest thing you could ever see. There is only a handful of people in the world that will ever get to see that. Now, don't misunderstand me. Ever since the Challenger disaster, we have had a "Special Unit" that monitors the lift-offs. As I said, I have a top-level five security clearance.

seventeen

2001, September 11th

WORLD TRADE CENTER BOMBING.

(Show a news clip of the attack on the towers)

I'm 35 years old, and my net worth is over $270,000,000.

On my Harley Davidson, I am going to Atlantic Ave to have lunch. I go into the restaurant, sit at the bar, and a waitress comes to take my order.

Jerome

"Hi, what's your name?"

Waitress

"Amore"

Jerome

"AMORE"

Jerome

"Oh my, what a beautiful name, almost as beautiful as you, if that's even possible."

I continue to have lunch there almost every day for a couple of months until I get the courage to ask her out. She is 14 years younger than me, she says, and we have been dating for about six months.

Jerome

"Will you marry me, Amore?"

Amore

"Yes"

We decided to have the wedding in Sicily, Italy. Where her parents live and my family is from, my brother Anthony does the wedding, and Craig is my best man.

My family has a covenant tattoo on our back right shoulder blade. It is a cross with Jesus on it; he has angel wings spread out, and in one hand is holding the holly grail, and in the other is an A-K 47. I keep it covered most of the time to avoid people identifying me, but I'm at my wedding, and we're swimming in her parent's pool. Her father sees it, now mind you, just married his daughter, and he recognized the tattoo, "Oh Shit" what was I thinking? My grandparents are from Sicily; he knows who my family is. I guess he saw how much we were in love and shrugged it off; he knew I would take good care of her. We shook hands the next morning before we went on our honeymoon, and I said,

Jerome

"Thank you"

He knew I wasn't talking about the wedding.

We went to Turks and Caicos for our honeymoon, where I own a home on the ocean. My daughter comes along; she and my now wife have become best friends.

We got invited to a concert in Saudi Arabia by King Abdulla (I met him by brokering an oil deal between our countries). He has nine wives and 31 children. I have a nanny working for my intel at his $740,000,000 home, the largest home in Saudi Arabia.

The heat was really on me now, so it was time for me to disappear for a while. So what we did was fake my death; I was just getting recognized by governments all around the world. My daughter set up a satellite so we could watch it and tape it. We needed to see if there were any suspicious persons at my funeral. After the funeral, my wife, daughter, bodyguard, and I go to my home in Colorado. The only way to get there was by helicopter. This is where I teach my daughter to shoot guns and handle weapons; she becomes a dead-on sniper. She can take out a target from over a mile away; this is also where I teach her survival skills.

(show this on screen)

Jerome

"Don't let the sun reflect off your scope. Take a position with the sun at your sides or back. Just take a deep breath, slowly exhale, and slowly exhale and relax your trigger finger. See the bullet hit the target in your mind and fire."

The bullet pierces the target dead center; she's ready now.

My father had taught me all this stuff, and I was a black belt by the time I was 12 years old.

My daughter will become my tech support, and we will get an assignment in Tokyo, Japan. We have a man who is stealing documents from one of our defense contractors. My helicopter picks us up and takes us to the Denver airport, where my jet is waiting for us. We arrived in Tokyo, and I exited the plane while my daughter was still on it. She now has me and my target on satellite. I proceed to the target with her help directing me to the target. I place 5 pounds of plastic explosives beneath the target's car.

Jerome

"Okay, wait until the target gets clear of all civilians and hit the switch."

(Boom! The car explodes)

Pentagon, we are taking out a poppy field in Afghanistan to hit al-Qaeda in the wallet. They are making billions of dollars selling heroin to fund.

Their terrorism organization, and yes, we, the CIA, are buying and shipping heroin into the US for dollars to fund our special ops. Did you think our C.I.A. wouldn't want a part of a multi-billion-dollar industry?

My daughter is at the Pentagon in Washington, D.C. In the war room, she has her target on satellite.

Daughter

"This is Alpha Tango, Father; the target is marked; deploy a drone to take out the target, code name Alice in Wonderland."

General enters the room.

General

"How is your father?"

Daughter

"He's good."

General

"How is Amore and the baby?"

Daughter

"Good, but she's not a baby anymore."

General

"Yeah, they grow up way too fast, especially for us while we're trying to Save the world."

March 13th, 300 million dollars in art was stolen from the Isabella Johnson Museum in Paris, France—a man dressed as a policeman was seen outside the museum around 8:00 PM. Despite efforts from around the world by the French administration, no arrests have been made, and no works have been recovered. We had the floor plan of the building. We had the blueprints of the security system; after all, we are the C.I.A. I entered the building and spoke to the security guard.

Jerome

"We got a call from the fourth floor, and I have to go up and check it out."

Security Guard

"Okay, boss, we're closing for the night, so make it quick."

I go up to the first floor and take off my police uniform, and underneath it, I have a painter's suit on. I shove it in the toilet, close the lid, and walk back.

Down the stairs.

Security Guard

"Did you see the policeman up there?"

Jerome

"No, sir."

Now, my daughter is outside the back door of the van, and she hacked into the computer system and security system. We have control of the cameras of the entire place. We have eyes on everything.

Over the security guard's radio to the other security guard in the camera monitoring room.

Security guard

"I'm going to make my rounds and make it clear to turn on the full security system."

Security Guard two

"Roger that, let's close her down."

The security guard now goes up the stairs to look for the policeman.

Jerome

"I'm wired up to my daughter in the van."

Sweetie, lock the cameras in a frozen position now.

Daughter

"Cameras locked, Papa."

I simply took the painting off the wall and walked out the back door to the van.

Jerome

"Okay, turn 'em back on, honey."

And we drove off. I sold them the following day to a collector friend who had ordered them from me for $200,000,000. It was just that easy.

Delray Beach, FL. I'm on Atlantic Ave, leaving the bar, driving my Harley at a stoplight. There is a police car behind me. I light up the bike and am smoking the tire. The cop behind me lights up his cherries, and I pull over as the police approach me. There is a whistle from an officer across the street.

"He's with me."

The officers return to their vehicle and drive off.

Back at the house the following day, I get my orders. My daughter and I headed to my jet and made the trip to Switzerland—time to go to work.

Bruno, a Swiss-born biochemist and associate of Carlos the Jackel, was last seen on a ferry from Italy to Greece on November 12th, 1999. He is thought to have been murdered as a body that was found might have been his, but authorities remain uncertain he was missing his fingers and teeth. Fortunately for him, he was a defector to the United States, and our job was to return him safely.

Our next assignment was in Israel. Mahmoud Atlaa, an alleged militant from the Pakistan Liberation Organization, was sentenced to jail in October 1997 and was later found not guilty and released sometime after he disappeared. He was believed to have participated in the attack on the World Trade Center towers in 2001 but was revealed not to have. We picked him up and brought him to Guantanamo Bay for more questioning. Later, we exonerated him, brought him to the U.S., and put him on the witness protection program to help us with information leading to the assignation of Assad Bin Lauden.

Now, I take my family on my jet to a business conference in Mexico City, Mexico. While I was attending my meeting, my wife and kids got kidnapped while out shopping. They were not supposed to leave the hotel until I returned, so it was time to go to work for my seal team; along with the support of the entire U.S. government, I got on a motorcycle, rode into the jungle roads and was captured by the guerilla forces. I pretended to be a journalist and wanted to interview the General of the opposition; it would be to their benefit for me to get their story out. I was handcuffed and had a hood put over my head. Now, I acted like I didn't speak any Spanish.

"No comprenda, no comprenda"

But I really understood everything they said. I am just waiting to hear anything they say about my wife and daughter. We went for days deep into the jungle, and I was held as a captive overnight at a couple of different camps. There were times when I thought for sure they were going to kill me. One of the soldiers put a gun to my head and pulled the trigger, but the gun was unloaded, so finally, we got to the main camp, and I was introduced to the General. I played out to be a journalist, and he ate it up. I manipulated him to think he was going to be a big star; he had no idea how dangerous I was, and they gave me my equipment back; my camera was equipped with a 38-caliber gun. I have cyanide caps disguised in my ink pens. I'm ready to kill all these mothers fuckers, but I'm helpless until I locate my family. That's when I overheard them talking about hostages coming to the camp, and they were waiting for a 5,000,000 ransom. Now, remember I have in my possession my credit card-sized transmitter device that I got at my conference, which is the reason I came here in the first place.

There they were, my wife and daughter, pulled into the campsite in a truck. They had hoods over their heads and didn't see me; I immediately deployed my GPS balloon to let my team get my coordinates. Now, I just had to wait; they would be parachuting in as soon as the night fell. We successfully killed everybody in the camp and returned to the U.S. safely. At this point in my life, I was becoming more of an ambassador diplomat for the U.S.A. instead of a target killer. The company for which I went to the conference had developed a tiny starlight balloon that, if you went down in a plane or shipwreck or for any reason, you got out of position in the middle of nowhere. I could deploy the ballon and get satellite coordinates, the communication of our position to be rescued. We gave our coordinates and an actual cell phone connection to anyone who had to contact us. It was the size of a credit card, so it would fit in your wallet, and it would end up saving a lot of lives and the recovery of our soldiers who were missing in action.

So now I have been assigned as head of South American Ops. I have a SEAL team directed under me, so I take my family and friends on my $40,000,000 yacht down to the Caribbean off the coast of Costa Rica. I opened a dummy corporation and created a salvage company as a cover for us. Now, my daughter and I started doing research for sunken ships in the area, as well as getting satellite images to search for sunken treasures. Now, sweep over these areas; you see all these dark spots underwater. They gotta be shipwrecks looking in accordance with some of these dark spots. We took the ship down there to investigate. My research shows there are several big-money wrecks down there; it's a perfect cover for us to operate. My daughter has located a few sites that we could dive into. So, my SEAL team goes diving on one of the sites and finds gold, silver, and precious stones. We begin slowly recovering the treasures so as not to raise any suspicions. I go; we located the San Benito that went down in 1717, carrying $15 billion. We now become smugglers once again. Something I am quite good at.

We also located a large cocoa field and processing plant deep in the Colombian jungle. I'm calling in an air strike from our aircraft carrier in the area.

Jerome

"Okay, guys, time to get suited up."

"Communication check diver one check."

Diver one

"Check, check."

"check, check."
"check, check."

It's taken over a year now to recover the treasures from the dive and get them back to the U.S., and now we don't have to worry about money ever again.

My wife has been singing in the church choir since she was 7 years old. She is a singer-songwriter, so I had a recording studio set up in my house. While we were in the Caribbean, she recorded her first album, and it went straight to the top. We are going on a world tour once again; I have a great cover to conduct my business.

UFO investigations. I had the opportunity to see it. I got called in for a crash landing of a UFO to secure the area. I was out on the ocean about 20 miles out offshore, and my people had GPS on my craft; they knew I was pretty close to the crash site. There were six crafts all lined up together in 2 rows; I buzzed over, and there was debris floating; a navy ship was there in about 20 minutes. The Coast Guard dropped five divers on my craft and told me ships were on the way soon; as they arrived, they dismissed me. Soon, as they went to another location, the black suits interviewed me, and they said nothing showed on the radar.

That was the last I heard about it. This is how it went:

Jerome

"Amore, amore, amore, come here, come here! Oh my God!

Amore

"I'm here, I'm here."

Jerome

"Oh my God, do you see this?"

"Come here. (holding hands) I don't fucking believe it."

Phone rings

Amore

"It's beautiful."

Jerome

"Amore, go beneath deck now. Hello, this is Jerome."

Caller

"Jerome, we got your coordinates on GPS. We're getting calls from ships out there in your area. What's going on out there?"

Jerome

"We have some airships out here, and I don't think they're ours."

Caller

“Stand by, we've already deployed assistance.”

Jerome

“Thank you, dispatch.”

Amore

“Honey, who was that?”

Jerome

"I told you to get below deck.”

Amore

“I’m just seeing if you are okay. I’m scared.”

Jerome

“I’m ok, sweetie. Just do what I say, please.”

Shzoom! Two F-16s fly over us. I go below deck and say,

Jerome

"It’s ok, doll. It’s just our military playing with their toys.”

Our next assignment was one of our agents who went rogue and was selling secrets to Russia; our mission was to locate the target and eliminate it. So, as they say, 'follow the money,' my daughter hacked into almost every bank in the world. We were looking for large deposits and then researching the people who made them, as well as any wire transports from Russia. Once we located him in Australia, we flew to Sidney. I brought my seal team on this one; we wanted to interrogate him, and I needed to know if he gave out the names of any of our agents; we took him to Guantanamo Bay, and I drove 2-inch nails into his head until I got what I was working for.

"Okay, okay."

Jerome

"Corporal, make a list, write everything down, and bring it to my office. I want it in five minutes, or I will be back to pound three more nails into his head."

Corporal

"Yes, sir."

I leave the room and go to my office. Within five minutes, the corporal hands me a piece of paper.

Jerome

"Corporal, take him to the enfermery."

Corporal

"Yes, sir."

My wife is doing a concert for the troops in Afghanistan. While she is working, my daughter and I go to work.

Jerome

“Okay, you get this one, baby girl. Do you see the one over there on the tree line ?”

“That’s where they will be hiding; they were shooting our marines from there today. Okay, there is one of them.”

“Do you see him?”

Daughter

“Yes.”

Jerome

"Ok, you get this one, he’s about 9000 kilometers North, wind speed 20 miles per hour, out of the North.”

Daughter

“Okay, I'm firing!” (bang)

Jerome

"Take the shot, okay? One-half meter to the right."

Daughter

"Okay," next shot (bang).

Jerome

"You got him, nice shot; we got another guy walking towards him. Take the shot. (bang)

Daughter

"Got him."

Jerome

"Nice shot, that's two confirmed kills; congratulations, you just saved a lot of marines."

On Radio

"Two for 'pick-up operations,' fox trot."

Jerome

"Roger Fox Trot"

On Radio

"He's on the ridge, copy?"

Jerome

"Roger, copy that."

Helicopter

Radio chatter

"Let's go home; it's a lot more funner than working at the Pentagon, huh?"

Jerome

"Yes, sir."

Brandy Britloa, one of the escorts employed by the D.C. madams, was a former professor at the University of Maryland who also committed suicide before she went to trial. Are you fucking kidding me? A woman of that stature committed suicide.

Okay, now let me get this straight: the original news came out stating the F.B.I. had a book of lists of all the madams' clients, then two weeks later, they discovered her hanging in the shed at her mother's home in Panallis County, FL. The news was worse when writing the following story that she threatened to give up the names in the book if she was prosecuted. They originally said the FBI had the book. Now, it's reported that she committed suicide, and there is no more mention of the book. What? Do all the Stupid people in this country have short-term memory loss? The whole thing became a cover-up to protect the guilty politicians, then faded into the forgotten past and was covered up with another news story to subside the lack of interest in this matter; both of these women were murdered.

Well, doesn't the FBI have... What is the client list, as they reported in the first place? It's funny how the population believes the news. Well, anyway, my name was in that book of clients, so use your imagination to figure out what really happened.

So when I was in the mountains in Afghanistan, I got bit by a wood tick, carrying Lyme disease and infected. I had it checked out by the field nurse first and the doctor next. When I got back to the States, I went to my doctor and many other specialists, and when I told them I got bit by a wood tick, and I think I got Lyme disease, I have all the symptoms. They all said I was crazy. Lyme disease is not real, so in turn, I got really, really sick from it. Untreated, it fucked up my nervous system so bad when I have bad days; all I want to do is kill myself, not just because of the brutal, brutal pain, the disease also messes with your psychological well-being, and the symptoms are homicidal and suicidal thoughts. I never had the homicidal part, but I fight immensely with suicidal thoughts, and maybe that's just because of my job.

Yeah, it blows my mind that a little bug could fuck my life so bad. I guess, in a way, it's God getting even with me for all the bad shit I've done in my life. I always thought I had a deal with

God, not a deal with the devil. So, I accept my punishment. And I will absorb all the pain and suffering for all the pain and suffering of the world.

www.ingramcontent.com/pod-product-compliance
Lightning Source LLC
LaVergne TN
LVHW040943150826
845672LV00002B/506

9798896913894